Tales of Wisdom and Truth:

Modern Life and Voices from the Past

Richard Grawath

I dedicate this book to my parents.

Published by Richard Grawath

ISBN 978-1-4717-4695-6

Tales of Wisdom and Truth:

Modern Life and Voices from the Past

Author Information

RG worked as a consultant, banker, analyst, researcher, teacher and university lecturer.

His qualifications provide the basis for his scientific and professional work:

Postgraduate Dip. in Medical Physics, M.Sc. in Science, M.B.A., Dip. in Psychology, B.Sc. (Honours) in Health Studies, B.Sc. (Honours) in Health & Social Care, University Cert. in Managing Care, University Cert. in Promoting Health, University Cert. in Reflective and Evidence-Based Practice, University Cert. in Health & Social Care.

Description

This book is about lost wisdom. In modern life many people have a superficial existence and the spiritual aspects of human life are often neglected. Religious and philosophical communities rarely provide real spiritual support. The feeling of emptiness has led individuals to search for meaning in consumption of physical and religious products. Many people hear about crimes against humanity but fail to point at the culprits and also fail to demand justice.

Table of Contents

Preface

The chapters of this book appear to be very different but they belong together and they centre around humanity, wisdom and freedom.

The extensive loss of wisdom is key to understanding current global developments in politics, economics, finance and societies.

The modern world in which we live is ultimately organised by a few people who can be identified by their pathological greed and lust for power.

In the annotations I draw sketches about the backgrounds of my tales, and my opinions are based on common sense, and scientific and historic facts.

I refer to scientific literature so that readers are able to check the facts and draw their own conclusions.

The combination of the different parts of this book is unusual but all these parts are connected through the themes mentioned above and each part contributes to a deeper understanding of the underlying themes in the modern world.

In this work I integrate art, literature, philosophy, science, history and politics.

My scientific comments in the annotations to the

short stories and to the review contain examples and the list could easily be extended. The annotations provide background information.

Our lives are very different from the lives of our parents and grandparents but these changes are not necessarily progress. The exposure of humans to toxins has increased over the last few decades and could easily be substantially reduced or even be completely prevented.

The picture of the book cover shows ruins of a lost civilisation in Cambodia and I am standing in front of theses ruins asking myself why this civilisation has disappeared. The ruin is part of the temples of Angkor which still look majestic and somehow express holiness. Nature reclaims the place and in the end, nature wins.

What will be left when we are gone? The ugliness of modern monstrosities, such as the Centre Pompidou in Paris or the modern Lloyd's building in London is in sharp contrast to the beauty of buildings from past époques such as the Alexander Palace in Russia, Sans Souci in Germany, Notre-Dame in Paris and the Acropolis in Athens. Visitors from outer space, assuming they exist just for the purpose of this theoretical discourse, may wonder whether the ugliness in areas of modern life has been created by the same species as the beauty of the past.

So far modern society has produced a lot of ugliness, and mountains and rivers of toxic waste. Solving environmental problems is not a matter of artificially regulating the size of the world population but of wise use of natural resources. We have to make sure that humans will rediscover humanity, including beauty, empathy and the right proportions in every area of modern life.

September 2020

Richard Grawath

r.grawath@mailfence.com

My Painting 'Lost Wisdom'

© Richard Grawath

My painting shows the head of a Buddha statue lying in the sand as the result of a brutal attack against the statue. When I travelled in Asia I saw many Buddha statues which had been decapitated. For me this expresses disrespect towards religions and philosophies of other people. It is also ignorance towards wisdom of the past. Talking to people who have different opinions and accepting other views is a prerequisite for understanding different cultures.

Dust

It was a cold winter night and I woke up feeling the cold creeping slowly into my body. I lifted the duvet and it had almost no weight at the top. I looked at it and at the bottom of the duvet there was a bulge while on the top I could only feel the cloth but nothing else.

I thought that I should buy some new feathers and add them to the duvet so that it would do a better job of protecting me against the cold. I decided to open the duvet and keep the good feathers while discarding the broken ones.

I opened the duvet very carefully and looked inside. There was only dust, no feathers, not even broken parts of feathers. There was nothing but dust. Now I could also see that the material of the cover was very brittle and the inside seemed to have more wear and tear than the outside. The material was red, two types of red, a dark red background with thin light red stripes.

I remembered my mother who cherished the duvet because it was the only thing she had from her childhood. I was just a few years old when she told me that the duvet came from an ancestor. At that age I was not interested in duvets but I remember her telling me that the people called our ancestor the 'Federjud'. I asked her what a 'Federjud' was and she explained to me that he was a Jew who collected feathers for duvets and pillows and that's why he was called the 'Federjud'. He collected feathers for a living. I asked no further questions.

Nothing more was left from the items of my ancestor but dust and a brittle red cover. I suddenly had a creepy feeling of guilt that I had not asked my mother questions about my ancestor when I was a child. Who was my ancestor? What kind of job was this collecting of feathers? My mother could not answer these questions any more as she had died much too early.

I remembered an old picture depicting Jewish people walking on a street, snow was lying on the street and the people were wearing thick coats. I could see that the coats had seen better days.

These people were not just walking along the street, most of them were carrying something and all of them appeared to be busy.

The duvet had certainly survived the First and the

Second World Wars. As a young woman my mother had escaped from Eastern Europe to the West and all the way she had this duvet with her. She had to hide in the fields and cross borders at night. She had to buy food on the black market and smuggle items across different sectors from different armies.

I asked myself what should I do with the dust? Surely it was impossible for me to throw the dust in the bin with the household rubbish. The dust was the only thing I had left from my ancestor so I had to find a solution which would allow me to feel good about the action taken.

I lived in a sleepy village where people watched everyone and everything. Nothing was private but I considered the disposal of the duvet as a private matter.

I decided to go to the forest where I knew a suitable place. During spring and summer, when the weather was dry and warm, teenagers used to meet there for romantic purposes. I discovered the place while I was walking with my dog. It was a small place hidden in the bushes and trees but not far away from the main path through the forest. I had seen colourful blankets shimmering through the leaves and I saw several young couples on blankets when I went closer to investigate the unusual colours.

A few days later on a late afternoon I folded the duvet and put it in a bag. The dog was jumping with excitement when I took the lead and we went off to the forest.

When I arrived at that place in the forest I unfolded the duvet and emptied the dust through the opening onto the ground. I let the brittle cover slide to the ground and the cover was lying there resembling mountains and valleys of an imaginary landscape. I left the scene with the feeling that I had done the right thing.

The restless wind played with the dust and then the dust returned to earth like planets returning to their origin.

The following spring and summer were wet and stormy so that I did not venture back into the forest for several months.

At the end of that year I took the dog out for a long walk and we went to that particular place in the forest.

The heap of dust had disappeared and so had the brittle cover but I could see a short piece of red thread. The thread was entangled with the branches of a shrub so that it would not be blown away by the wind. The thread had retained a little bit of its original red colour. The red thread may have been used for a repair at some point in time after the duvet had been created.

The Five Monks

Lisa was in her late fifties. Her wrinkly skin covered her scull in a way that her face looked bony. Her brown eyes were sitting deep in their sockets and were surrounded by dark coloured skin. Looking at her gave one the impression that time had left marks of a hard and demanding life on her face.

She was wearing earrings which were stretching the holes in her earlobes so that the holes were elongated.

Until recently she had worked as a teacher of different business subjects. Now she felt emptiness and she was lonely. She decided to try writing something but her only story was the story from her previous life. She developed a plan. She would ask people she knew who had a solid background in science to answer questions and then she would write these answers down and then she would pretend that these thoughts were her thoughts. She would publish these thoughts from other people under her name on her website and this would create traffic to her website so that she would be able to commercially use this. This should help her to earn money.

There was a scientist who had realised that Lisa just asked him questions about science so that she could publish his answers in her name without making reference to him. As a consequence he stopped answering her questions so she simply told him that she was not going to share her publications with him. She had thought this through: Even if the scientist were to ask a lawyer to find Lisa and challenge her, what would happen? She would not pay a penny even if the lawyer would find her. How could anyone find her? She would be constantly on the move, living with one person until she was thrown out and then she would live with the next person and so on.

Lisa decided to move out of her apartment and live with people whom she had befriended for that purpose. She thought: 'How silly these people are. They believe that I am their friend just because I am friendly with them. They don't understand that I want to live in their apartments free of charge. I will tell them lies so that they don't get the idea that I am playing with them. The sillier the lie the better. I'll tell them that I want to live in a cave and they'll feel pity for me.'

Lisa's husband did not understand her anymore. Her husband left her after she refused to consult a psychiatrist. She did not accept that the physical world could help her to find answers to her questions. This situation with her husband had been going on for years. Her husband tried to reason with her and he arranged appointments with several psychiatrist but she would not go to any professional.

For Lisa there was much more to life than just the superficial world with all its trappings. Most people just got trapped in modern society. They did not understand the spiritual dimensions. Lisa's son also talked to her but this was just to support the arguments of her husband. Who was he to talk to her like that? He was an adult but he was her son, so what did he know about life? He did not understand her thoughts about the immaterial dimensions and the spiritual world which held the keys to the questions which had plagued Lisa for years.

Lisa paid for a meditation course because she was looking for answers to her questions. There in the temple in India she met people who understood her and encouraged her to explore her past. She lived in the temple for three months and got advice from the monks. She revisited her past life in which she had provided pleasure for men who came to the temple.

Without the monks Lisa would not have been able to discover her past life but now she could not reconcile the gap between her time as a temple dancer seven-hundred years ago and her current life. She must have been reborn again and again but as what and where? The monks were of great help to her when she tried to relive her experience of remembering her life as a temple dancer. Lisa suddenly felt the creativity she had had seven-hundred years ago when she was a temple dancer in India.

Now she could not be a temple dancer because she was too old but she felt the desire to do something creative and to earn money without the hassle of modern life as a teacher in a school or even working in an office. She needed money to pay the monks and for the mushroom drinks. The mushroom drinks had opened a usually hidden area to her and she needed to know more about her previous lives.

One of the monks gave Lisa a big cup with the

mushroom drink and she was told that this concoction would enable her to access information about her previous lives. Lisa greedily emptied the cup, leaving not a drop of the precious fluid. Lisa made herself comfortable on the floor. There she was as nature had intended her to be and her skin was ready to experience the slightest touch. The world around her started to move, the colours intensified and suddenly the world disappeared in a hole which was surrounded by darkness. She entered the hole in a spiral motion. There was a voice talking to her but the sound was muffled, as if the speaker was far away and as if the speaker was talking behind a thick curtain. The voice told her that she was a temple dancer in India, a long time ago, a very long time ago, as long as seven-hundred years ago. Lisa was moving. Her body was gliding along the floor and the five monks touched her body. Their hands were floating over her body, exploring her cavities, entering them and sliding out again.

Their bodies made contact and energy was pulsating from one body to another, similar to an electric spark flying from one body to the next.

Again and again and again she felt the penetrating

pleasure which was mixed with the effects of the mushroom drink but she did not hear the voice again. Now there was no voice to tell her more about her previous lives. The voice was absent despite her repeated attempts to enter other dimensions and to obtain more information about her previous lives. The voice had disappeared.

The Node and a Step Stone to Hell

During the 3rd Reich Wuppertal was a node in the railway network that covered the whole of Germany. At that time undercover agents, in particular the Gestapo, would board trains and buses looking to arrest people whom they suspected of not being in line with the Nazi's irrational and inhumane race laws.

Unfortunately, there are many wicked people following the same principles and practising the same methods in Wuppertal today...

It was a cold and rainy day and I decided to use the monorail. The monorail ran over the river Wupper right through the town of Wuppertal. Wuppertal had its heyday as an industrial city in Germany at the beginning of the 20th century, but it has been in decline for many decades.

I purchased a ticket from a ticket machine and then entered the train. The doors closed and the train started to move. A few seconds later some of the new passengers began to blare out: "Ticket control! Ticket control!"

The ticket controllers were working undercover,

which meant that they were disguised as ordinary passengers. One of these new passengers came up to me. I looked at him and I knew that he was a controller.

"During the 3rd Reich the Gestapo used the same methods," I said "sneaking around undercover in trains and buses and then checking up on people. This is the same mentality. Considering what the Nazis did to the world you should be ashamed of yourself. You should be more sensitive in this respect."

The controller ignored me and went on to the women sitting next to me. She opened her purse and showed him her ticket. Then he spotted a whole pile of used tickets in her purse.

"You have to give me your old tickets," he said. "They are the property of the Public Transportation Department."

The woman avoided the controller's eyes. "I have kept them because I am on a low income," she said quietly. "I get a refund when I hand them in to my employer at the end of the month. If I give the old tickets to you I won't get the refund and I won't have enough money to feed my children."

The controller was unmoved by her explanation.

"I already told you," he said, "the tickets are the property of the Public Transportation Department. Give them to me or I will call the police." She hesitated, and he increased the pressure, "You'd better hand them over to me right now or there will also be additional charges of disrupting the orderly running of a public transport system."

At this point in time the commotion had attracted the attention of the other controllers who intimidated the woman further by surrounding her and staring at her. Then the woman began to cry and I said to her, "I will give you my telephone number so that you can call me. I am prepared to act as a witness for you in a court hearing. I have already made a note about the aggressive and threatening behaviour of the controllers."

Now the first controller tried to intimidate me. "I will prosecute you as well," he warned. "You will be in a lot of trouble. I shall order the police to search you on the spot and then take you to the police station together with this woman."

I was quite confident that this was an empty threat and I stared him in the eye. "Oh, I am so looking forward to the court hearing. My lawyer will question you about this," I answered.

The controller had not expected another passenger to intervene. First he hesitated and grinned at me. Then he raised his right arm, stretching it out in front of him. "I am just searching for the handrail to hold on, although you might think I am doing something different." Then he clicked his heels together. "In the past we had very effective methods of dealing with people like you," he whispered. "History repeats itself but this time we'll win. No one will be able to sabotage us a second time."

No sooner had he spoken then the train stopped at a station. Without another word, he turned and disappeared onto the platform.

One of the passengers looked at me. "I am very proud of what my grand-father did during the 3rd Reich," he said.

I looked at him and replied, "Do you mean killing tens of millions of people worldwide and all the destruction?"

None of the other passengers bothered to comment. I left the train at the next station and headed for a coffee shop.

An elderly woman entered the coffee shop. She was wearing a red jacket and dark blue trousers. Her hair was dark chestnut brown and thick, so thick you could not see her hairline.

The coffee shop was self-service. She helped herself to a cup of coffee, put a cake on her tray and then started looking around for somewhere to sit. She spotted me alone at a table and came over to me, but because I was busy writing on my laptop I didn't pay her much attention.

"Is this seat free?" she asked. Her German had a very strong accent.

I looked up, surprised. "Yes," I said. Without another word she sat down, but somehow I knew she wanted to talk.

"I can see that you are busy but may I ask you a question?" she asked a moment later.

I smiled. "Yes, of course."

She had seen my English newspaper on the table. "You are not from here, are you?" she asked.

Now I looked at her more closely. I noticed that her cheeks were powdered and rouged and she was wearing red nail polish. Then I saw her thin gold necklace with its Star of David pendant.

"No, I'm not from here. I'm just visiting a friend. I assume you're not from here either."

"No, I have never been here before. I'm a visitor too, but for a very different reason." She paused, looked at me for a while as if she was lost in thought, then she began…

"In the 1940s the Nazis put my uncle on a train to a concentration camp, but he disappeared before the train arrived at its destination. I have information from a survivor that my uncle was last seen at Wuppertal train station."

I sighed. Back then Wuppertal train station was on the path for trains which transported Jews to Nazi death camps.

"The citizens of Wuppertal had a very bad reputation in those days," she explained. "They used to open the railway trucks and beat the deportees with wooden sticks. Some of these Nazis threw stones and they enjoyed it when people were begged for water. People trying to escape were brutally beaten. Some were even beaten to death and the wardens just laughed."

Suddenly the woman stopped talking and she stared at me. "Wuppertal was a stepping stone to hell," she said finally.

I looked back at her. "I don't think you'll find any trace of your uncle here," I said, "nor will you find anyone here who was an eyewitness or who is prepared to talk to you about this."

She nodded sadly. "Yes, I know. But that's not why I'm here. I'm here to see the people. I want to get a feeling for this place, to see if things have really changed."

She studied the scenery in the coffee shop. It seemed to be an ordinary day and ordinary people seemed to enjoy an ordinary cup of coffee. Then she was leaning forward across the table and whispered.

"This is a dying town. I can see some foreigners here, but I also see swastikas painted on the walls. Is this the famous writing on the wall?"

She did not wait for me to answer and leaned back in her chair. "But what about you?" she asked. "Why are you here?"

"I'm waiting for a friend. Now he's at a labour court. He came to Wuppertal about three years ago to take up a promising job offer. Right from beginning the company dangled a carrot in front of his nose: he would become head of the department when the current head would retire in two and a half years. Not long ago he was dismissed for no good reason, so he took the company to court. He's English by the way. He came here to Wuppertal because of this new job. He's not only highly skilled but also a hard worker. His colleague, a local woman, was on maternity leave most of the time, but when she finally returned to full-time work the company sacked my friend and hired two Germans in his place."

The woman shook her head. "Wuppertal isn't a small place by German standards," she said. "Can a whole city be racist?"

"I don't know. I just think that Wuppertal still has a very high percentage of Nazi supporters, but I guess there are some decent people here too."

I don't think I sounded very convincing. I had already heard local people make derogatory comments about Jews and the locals didn't like me either because it was obvious to them that I wasn't one of them.

"It's sad but after the war Nazis were able to get leading positions in governments at all levels in West Germany," I said, "and also in most of the big companies. They hide behind rules and regulations and try to harass anyone they don't like in order to pursue their nasty ideas. They're no different from the Nazis of the 3rd Reich."

The woman chewed her lip but didn't say anything.

"Yesterday evening there was a demonstration against Holocaust deniers in the market place in front of the town hall, but it was just a small group of demonstrators" I explained. "The demonstration was not violent, but the demonstrators had to adopt a defensive strategy. It is scary that the Nazis and Fascists here are not afraid to speak out. No one does anything substantial against the Nazis. Why don't the town's leaders do something about it? It's because so many local people support these evil people, that's why. Having *Stolpersteine* to remember Jewish victims is a good idea but the idea of putting *Stolpersteine* in the pavement is not based on the initiative of a politician."

The woman was listening intently.

"Yes, this is modern Wuppertal," she said gloomily. "From what you've just said it's no different from the old Wuppertal."

She looked out of the window, seemingly to collect

her thoughts. When she looked back at me her face was set and determined.

"I survived the Holocaust," she said. "But I was lucky. I was a nurse then and they needed nurses in the concentration camps. I worked as a dental assistant. The dentist was a young woman, an Aryan, as the Nazis would say. She was also a devil in a white coat. She pulled out gold teeth without anaesthesia. But if that didn't produce enough pain for her she'd put salt on the wounds. The poor patients were screaming in agony and there was nothing I could do to help them. I can still hear their screams....I can't sleep, I can't forget, I can't rest. Oh, those screams... the memories…"

The woman stopped speaking and brought her hands to her face.

I had heard many similar stories about the dark days of World War II from other Holocaust survivors and even from ordinary Germans.

The woman made an effort to gather herself and then she looked at me again. "But worst of all, after the liberation this dentist claimed that she used the salt to close the wounds in order to prevent infection. She was allowed to practise again as a dentist, and she went to a city in the north of Germany where she earned a fortune. I made a statement to the authorities about what she had done, but no one wanted to listen. She did terrible, terrible things and got away with it? How did she do that? I don't understand…"

"Maybe everyone wanted to forget. Maybe everyone wanted to believe the excuses. After the 3rd Reich, even Kurt Georg Kissinger, a chancellor of West Germany was a former member of the Nazi party."

She didn't know that. She looked shocked.

"What? You mean a Nazi was head of the German government after the war?"

"Yes."

"So that means that he supported Hitler and was then elected chancellor? How could that happen?"

"Oh, that was easy," I said. I knew all about Kurt Georg Kissinger. "After the war he was a member of the Christian Democratic Party. Nazis like him had many excuses for what they had done and the allies were only too willing to believe their stories. Better an ex-member of the Nazi party than a communist, I suppose. And when the old Nazi bureaucrats retired after the war they made sure that their positions were filled with like-mined cronies. This is also probably why so many locals in Wuppertal are still racists."

The woman looked at me. "Yes," she said, "ghastly actions of the Nazis were possible because good people did not act, did not even say anything.... Evil has to be opposed when it happens, right from the beginning, long before it gains ground."

A Review: Paul Kuttner: An Endless Struggle

Kuttner, Paul. *An Endless Struggle*. 1st. Edn.: Vantage Press Publ., 2010. ISBN 978-0-533-15498-2.

Kuttner wrote his book in an interesting way and each chapter is a unit.

As a teenager Kuttner lived in pre-war Germany in Berlin. This was the centre of the 3rd Reich and there he met Hitler, Goering and other high-ranking Nazi criminals. Kuttner escaped the Holocaust, and he experienced England at war. Later Kuttner moved to post-war USA. Kuttner's life in the US epitomises the lives of many decent people in Western democracies who work hard just to stay above water.

Kuttner acquired a unique set of experiences by living in four different worlds (Berlin, London, Hollywood, New York City), and he writes about his experiences in an interesting narrative style.

The phrase 'production of knowledges' as it is used in discursive psychology came to my mind while I was reading Kuttner's book. It might appear unusual to use the plural of knowledge, but the plural is used to indicate that there is more than just one truth.

Kuttner's experiences strongly influenced his definitions and meanings.

Kuttner critically evaluates long-term developments when he refers to relatively recent political issues. This is wisdom which can rarely be observed.

I am sure that Kuttner's book can help to answer questions which we cannot even contemplate at the moment. In the future researchers might be interested in a particular aspect of the historic events described in Kuttner's book.

Kuttner's book is very much about interactions between people, and history books notoriously lack this kind of knowledge. Kuttner is an eyewitness who is able to describe his living conditions in Nazi Germany. Kuttner's text reveals how innocent individuals and groups were singled out and trapped in a brutal control system by the Nazis.

Kuttner's story is interwoven with big history. It is not only the important historical setting which makes his book interesting to read; it is also that I can see the emotions and feelings of many other individuals who are actors in the scene.

Kuttner has met many famous people, but this is only one part of his story. Kuttner provides many names, and this indicates who influenced him and his peers.

In fact, over large passages of this book I got the feeling that the author is talking to me.

Annotations

Annotations to 'Lost Wisdom'

The title 'Lost Wisdom' refers to the fact that the technocrats and other groups are detached from wisdom, in particular wisdom of the past. The technocrats and other groups are not aware that wisdom is essential for the survival of mankind.

Humans have limitations and recognising these limitation enables individuals to live free and satisfying lives. The power and magnitude of nature will always be above anything created by humans no matter how advanced the technology will be. Humans may be able to manipulate parts of certain sections of the environment, such as a local area of the sea, but the magnitude of all water on Earth will never be under the absolute control of humans. This is the key issue. Some individuals may think that they can exercise total control over nature, but all human science, construction and engineering have limitations.

The scientific method acknowledges that scientific hypotheses are not absolute knowledge. Scientific hypotheses are certainly no wisdom. Positivism assumes that objectivity exists but other philosophical approaches to science dispute this assumption [1]. According to Karl Popper a scientific study should have a design which allows to falsify hypotheses which, in turn, serves the task of rejecting wrong theories [1]. In Popper's approach theories are never final because if a theory is true then science is not able to know that this is the final absolute truth [1]. As a consequence, new theories develop based on new observations and interpretations. In this context science and politics may follow an identical principle.

Probabilities are at the centre of statistics when it comes to decision making and there is uncertainty about events to occur [2]. Confusion and errors in concepts do occur in science [3].

The assumption of the dualists that the human brain is simply matter and the mind is immaterial causes a basic scientific problem [4]. If the mind has no material nature then scientific investigations about the mind face the problem that scientific laws generally used to explore matter do not apply [4]. There is no commonly accepted definition of the mind and there is uncertainty about the location of the mind.

Explanatory gaps in the precise workings of the brain exist [4]. Neuronal activities, cognitive processes and consciousness interact with each other, but exactly how is still under investigation [4]. The brain makes decisions and it is also the origin of voluntary actions [3].

The activities of the autonomic nervous system are mainly involuntarily and there are close connections to the central nervous system [5]. In neurons there are both chemical and electric transmissions.

The heart possesses automaticity which means that neural impulses are generated within the heart [6]. The sinoatrial node is the pacemaker [6]. The atrioventricular node receives the impulses from the sinostrial node and there is a specialised conducting system [6]. This conducting system starts with the bundle of His and it continues with the two Tawara's bundle branches [6]. Next are the Purkinje fibres [6]. The vagus nerve has parasympathetic fibres which can modulate heart activity through the release of acetylcholine, thereby adjusting heart activity to current needs [6]. This is just one example how the brain is connected and works in a complex organic system which has to be understood in its entirety. The conditions, age and functioning of the organs can influence mood, happiness and mental health, just to name a few domains of psychology.

The brain is a vital organ and it is also highly susceptible to the lack of oxygen. Therefore the brain is number one on the list of all organs which have to be supplied with oxygen [6].

The vagus nerve fibres are so numerous that the knowledge of the extent of the distribution of all fibres is theoretical and not precise [7]. The vagus nerve is the tenth cranial nerve and all other cranial nerves are shorter [7].

The term 'inner world' is sometimes used for the limbic system which controls motivations, emotions and instinct behaviour [8].

The described situation shows that the brain is part of a whole organism. It depends on the functioning of other organs and it interferes with the functions of organs, even with the automaticity of the heart. It is important to note that there is input from the brain to the other parts of the body and there is output from other parts of the body to the brain.

The continuous, extensive and complex interactions

within the bodies of higher organisms, including humans, are part of life and are not part of an inanimate machine such as a computer. Neurons and other cells use an analogue electrical system whereas computers work with a digital system i.e. zero and one.

The resting potential between -50 and -100 mV of nerve and muscle cells is maintained when no stimulus exists and several processes are involved in maintaining the resting potential [9]. For skeletal muscles endplate potentials depolarise at about 70 mV, while neuronal excitatory postsynaptic potentials already depolarise at a few mV [9]. For glutamate the excitatory postsynaptic potential has a maximum of 20 mV [9]. There is also a time factor because the release of the neurotransmitter is relatively slow and also the diffusion of the neurotransmitter causes a delay for the excitatory postsynaptic potential [9]. The example of the resting potential and the other examples show that human neurons and other cells work in a completely different way and environment compared to a computer.

Subjectivity is an integral part of this complex living

system. Scientists conducting experiments may introduce subjectivity into their scientific investigations through various means, such as by selecting a particular subject, deciding a method of investigation, picking the timing or choosing a specific analysis method. In psychology scientific predicates concern the whole body, e.g., the eye is just one part of the visual system [3].

Dr Paul MacLean suggested that there are three brains in the human brain [10]. The brain contains the history of human evolution in three sections, the reptilian section, the mammalian section and the cerebral neocorteza section [10]. The subconscious part of the psyche is much larger than the conscious part [10]. The large extent of subconsciousness has long been known and it is an important insight from Sigmund Freud which he used in the development of his psychoanalysis.

In classical Chinese philosophy the harmony of functional systems working together is key for understanding humans [11].

Technocracy neglects these insights, experiences and the evolutionary inheritance of living humans which are at the centre of every human being.

In psychological experiments in implicit learning some researchers have computerised displays of stimuli but the screen refresh rate is a limitation [4]. Other limitations for computerized experiment setups exist.

Humans have the ability to learn even when they are not aware of a particular thing [4].

The theory that bodies are just biological machines is still the orthodox belief system in science and medicine [12]. In contrast to technocrats who may believe that they can understand and can impose complete control over humans, it is probably impossible to understand the human in its entire complexity.

Dictates of the technocrats have already been implemented, such as biometric passport pictures, digitalised fingerprinting for passports, iris scans and so-called gender neutral language. These dictates completely ignore that language is the product of historical processes and that grammatical gender has nothing to do with biological sex.

In the German language most nouns are feminine. The group of masculine nouns is much smaller and the group of neutral nouns the smallest group. The

German word for girl is 'Mädchen' and in terms of grammar this word is neutral in the same way the word window is neutral, namely 'Fenster'. In French, the word 'girl' (fille) is feminine whereas the word for 'window' (fenêtre) is masculine. The word uterus is masculine in the German language despite it being part of the female sex organs and here it is important to note that 'der Uterus' has the Latin word ending -us. In general, Latin words ending in –us are male regardless of the meaning of the word. This shows that grammatical genders do not follow any scientific gender logic.

Introducing artificial changes into a language may break the flow of the language and may create ugliness. This ugliness may alienate individuals from their mother tongue and even though this might not be a conscious experience a loss of identity may also occur.

The disputes about grammatical gender are just a distraction from the real problems such as synthetic biology, trans-humanism and other disastrous inhuman concepts.

This is the old strategy of divide and conquer.

In the USA there are about 50 large research universities which have huge budgets and colossal endowments [13]. In 2005 Stanford University had a USD 2.9 billion budget in addition to a capital budget of USD 373 million and an endowment of USD 12.2 billion [13]. Foundations which do not have to pay taxes have to spend 5% of their endowments per year [13]. Universities do not have to comply with these federal regulations and the majority of them are spending below 5% of their endowments [13].

The tuition fees can be seen as taxes and the universities also have elections similar to a sovereign government [13]. Universities are sheltered from brutal properties of capitalism since tax exemptions, gifts from philanthropic institutes, private donations, state support and self-governed pricing provide them with a very good monetary climate [13]. Every year the physical and medical sciences university departments receive USD 30 billion from Washington D.C. [13].

The Onco-Mouse, a genetically modified mouse, was partially financed by DuPont which donated USD 6 million to Harvard [13]. In 1988 the Onco-Mouse was patented by Harvard. DuPont received an exclusive license and the arrangement was one of the largest of its kind between academia and the corporate world [13]. In a 1993 article the Onco-Mouse was described as a failure because DuPont could not sell a single license to a pharmaceutical company and DuPont stated that royalties could have been in the billions [14]. DuPont therefore dropped the original royalty for every pharmaceutical developed with the Onco-Mouse and revised the contract draft [14].

Strong criticism about the development of Genetically Modified (GM) animals and other GM organisms, in particular the Onco-Mouse, is based on ethical grounds, moral grounds and on questions about necessity and usefulness.

The scientific revolution of the Onco-Mouse has not produced the promised benefits for patients and it is unlikely that it will [15]. Furthermore other GM mouse models for Alzheimer's, respiratory and cardiovascular diseases have also failed to improve the outcomes of these major causes of morbidity and mortality of humans [15]. The vast sums of money spent on the fruitless research has channelled these enormous financial resources away from other more promising research [15].

Many pharmaceuticals which showed good results in GM mouse models did not only fail to do good but produced harm to patients who suffered from cancer, heart disease, Parkinson's disease and Alzheimer's [15]. The engineering of GM animals is facing many complications and it is not precise [15]. Epigenetics and the on-off switching of genes complicate the picture. Interactions between genes may also be more extensive and important than previously thought.

Some researchers may possess extensive overconfidence with respect to their insights and their scientific capabilities to control nature. I would like to introduce the term 'overconfidence disorder' for this extensive pathological overconfidence. It may also be observed in technocrats.

Universities and their science and medical research facilities receive large funds from governments and these funds are used for financing the research projects of for-profit companies which may only contribute relatively small amounts of money. Scholarships of various sources may also contribute indirectly to co-finance the R&D departments of for-profit companies. If a research project is a commercial success then it is more likely that the generated profit flows into the pockets of private owners, shareholders and upper management. Managers of for-profit companies are concerned about short-term profit which is more likely to benefit them in terms of remuneration and promotion. These managers are less concerned about wisdom or the production of knowledge which might deliver benefits for society.

Annotations to 'Dust'

This short story is not only about how I connect to my family's past; it is also about how people in the past lived as much as possible in harmony with nature. Items of daily life were made out of degradable materials which were given back to nature after use.

In contrast to widespread belief, duvets and pillows filled with feathers contain fewer house mite antigen particles than those filled with polyester [16].

In a study it was found that polyester used for the fillings of pillows showed as much as eight times the amount of mite antigen compared to feather fillings [16]. Findings from a different study show that fillings with processed feathers do not contain mite antigens [16].

Asthma due to mite antigens has a higher prevalence in economically developed countries compared to less developed countries [16]. Both primary and secondary prevention are key in asthma [16]. In light of prevention, previous generations ironed bed sheets and pillow cases and they usually aired out rooms twice a day [16]. This can be seen as wisdom based on experience and observation. Modern technology with air-conditioning and plastics everywhere struggles to keep up with the advice from the past which kept asthma caused by mite antigens down.

PVC-U, for example, can contain lead in its stabilising systems which are designed to prevent degradation when exposed to certain environmental conditions such as light. Lead poisoning may affect all organs and it is far more severe for children since children have not yet completed their development [17]. Lead may have been replaced by other chemicals because it is a heavy metal and toxic, but if the replacement is also toxic or carcinogenic then the replacement is just creating another problem. Cadmium is used in the production of PVC as a stabiliser [18]. The toxicity of cadmium has a wide spectrum as it interferes extensively with the mitochondria, the DNA, the cardio-vascular system, the reproductive system, certain enzymes and with other systems and processes [18]. This replacement of one highly toxic element with another highly toxic element is like jumping out of the frying pan directly into the fire.

During the production process of PVC dioxins and furans are formed [19]. Incomplete burning of waste, mainly plastic waste, also leads to the formation of dioxins [20]. Other fires with incomplete combustion, such as burning of municipal waste, household waste and agricultural fires produce dioxins [20]. Dioxins and furans cause a very heavy burden on the health of humans [19].

Polymers play a major part in fires in households, transportation and commercial settings [21].

According to the 2005 final report from the Office of Aviation Research, about 95% of all polymers in households, transportation and commercial settings are cheap, costing less than USD 1 per pound [21]. A tiny flame is sufficient to ignite these cheap polymers and they will continue burning even after the igniting source has been removed [21]. More expensive polymers tend to be more fire resistant because they are mostly fluoropolymers or contain aromatic backbones [21]. However, price does not always correlate with fire resistance and higher fire resistant polymers cost more than twice the price of the cheap plastics [21].

Ignition resistant, flame resistant and fire retardant

are terms which are tested under laboratory conditions [21]. This limits their meaning in the real world. Ignition resistance is an intrinsic property of special fire-resistant polymers and chemical additives may introduce fire resistant properties to a polymer which otherwise would not be classified as fire resistant [21]. Economic considerations have led research to focus on fire resistant additives rather than on research into fire resistance as an intrinsic property of a polymer [21].

Health and safety are not at the centre of decision making when it comes to deciding which material is used in a particular product.

In the car manufacturing industry a highly flammable element, lithium, is used for the batteries in electric cars regardless of the potential dangers for humans and the environment. In addition to these direct dangers for humans, the mining of the so called rare earth metals which are, for example, used as pigments in display screens of those cars and other products is not environmentally friendly and recycling of those elements is in its infancy. There is also the question how much of the electricity for the electric cars is really produced in an environmentally friendly way. In contrast to these facts, electric cars are presented as environmentally friendly.

The smoke of polymer fires contain complete combustion products, such as acid gases and carbon dioxide, and incomplete combustion products such as partially oxidised fuel gases, carbon monoxide and soot [21], carbon monoxide being considered the most toxic substance of the smoke [22]. Hull and Stec (2009) state that the majority of deaths during a fire is attributed to smoke inhalation [22].

The main hazard of polymer fires is the smoke produced which depends on chemical composition and ventilation of the place of fire [21].

PVC and wood have a very low burning rate compared to polymers with aromatic oxygen and nitrogen (Polyurethane ((PU)), PET, epoxy ((EP)), PBT, VE, PPO, bismaleimide) [21]. The natural polymers tend to have a lower flammability compared to the corresponding synthetic plastic such as polyethylene which has a caloric value close to petroleum [22].

The very low burning rate is accompanied by a low production of smoke as measured in unit mass of the particular material burned [21]. PPS and PSU are polymers which contain aromatic sulphur and they produce more smoke than wood or PVC [21]. Some aromatic polymers (EP, PS, ABS) produce up to 50% more smoke when flame retardants containing bromine are added [21].

Does it make sense to develop and use flame retardant additives which lead to an increase in smoke production instead of developing polymers which have fire resistance as an intrinsic property?

The dripping behaviour of polymers is also problematic. In one scenario dripping away may help to spread the fire while in another test ignitability may be reduced by dripping away when nanofillers have been added to the polymer [22].

The pyrolysis products of PVC are toluene, benzene and hydrochloric acid (HCl) whereas the pyrolysis products of cellulose are water, carbon dioxide and carbon monoxide [21]. The symptoms of toluene poisoning include renal failure, metabolic acidosis and liver injury [23]. Toluene and benzene belong to the group of hydrocarbons, all of which can cause dysrhythmia of the heart which is potentially life-threatening [24]. The hydrocarbons can also destroy the membranes of capillaries and alveoli [24]. In addition, benzene and toluene may cause other serious health damage [24]. HCl is also toxic and on exposure to it a person may experience irritation of the respiratory system and the eyes as well as corrosive effects on tissues [25].

The potentially very poisonous additives of PVC might not justify its widespread use.

PVC-U is widely used for example in window frames and when these frames are exposed to heat above 80 degrees centigrade then hydrochloric acid is formed and contaminates the walls of a building in the event of a fire. Small amounts of dioxins, which include the most toxic substances known to mankind, are also released in fires of modern houses containing many materials made of PVC. Those contaminated houses have to be professionally decontaminated before humans can move in again.

Considering how many modern houses are now heavily equipped with PVC, such as plastic window frames, other building materials containing PVC, furniture and decorations, it becomes clear that professional decontamination becomes a huge nightmare in events which are accompanied by fire blasts. The question has to be asked whether there are the technical capacities for urban areas to decontaminate these areas in the event of a fire blast or other serious emergencies. In times of war numerous urban areas may be under attack at the same time creating an even larger demand for decontamination from all sorts of chemicals, radioactive substances and biological weapons.

In addition to plastics, building materials such as granite may create a radioactive health hazard for the inhabitants since certain granites show relatively high radioactivity [26]. Even though granite has been used for thousands of years as a building material, nowadays granite is fashionable and the potential health hazard might therefore be more widespread than previously. Natural stones often contain radioactive isotopes but most of the time emit only very small amounts of radioactivity.

Exposure to radioactivity and other health hazards should be kept as low as possible. Accumulation of health hazards occurs as well as interactions of radiation, chemicals, biochemicals and organisms and this has unnecessarily drastically increased in modern times. I can only hope that there will never be an event in which these toxic and radioactive substances are pulverised and the resulting hazardous dust is released in a large scale event such as a war.

Annotations to 'The Five Monks'

In the current society rationalisation is worshipped like a god by technocrats and other like-minded groups. Rationalisation is a process in which emotions such as empathy are replaced by rational reasoning. Tradition and values, in particular ethical values, are also replaced. Technocracy uses rationalization, whereby gaps are deliberately created. These gaps in the psychological field remain open and need to be filled. There are several ways to fill theses gaps. Consumption is promoted by the current economic and financial system and by technocracy.

The use of smart phones has become an addiction. These devices promote passive consumption. Most people do not realise that smart phones are also tracking devices and are extensively used to channel thinking processes, i.e. brainwashing.

Standardisation and predictability of services appear to make life easier for manipulated individuals who are made to believe that technocratic procedures and systems serve their interests best. Control and calculability do serve certain groups but not the majority of people.

Humans are commercialised when their data are used to maximise profit and the humans are not even asked to agree. Loss of privacy is imposed through the mandatory use of bio-metrics, DNA profiling, vaccination, and tests.

Buddhist monks are expected to follow strict guidelines but the reality can be quite different. In Thailand scandals surrounding the clergy include money laundering, child abduction, child abuse and sexual assaults [27]. Some monks have been jailed for drug dealing and murder [27]. Unruly commercial activities of Buddhist monks in Thailand, such as fortune telling and selling luck-bringing amulets have also been observed [27]. In addition, there fake monks abusing the trust of people [28]. Thai Buddhist authorities have launched a hotline hoping this will help to improve the reputation of Buddhism [28].

In 2014 a military junta seized power in Thailand and started a crackdown on corruption which also included the Buddhist clergy [27]. The previous civil governments were reluctant to tackle corrupt clergy because there was a fear of losing votes since 95% of the population are Buddhists [27].

There are also reports about scandals in India where members of the Buddhist clergy are accused of all types of crimes, including physical and sexual abuse of children [29]. The Buddhist community is now confronted with severe scandals worldwide [29].

Commercialisation of religion is a two-way street, individuals expecting to buy something to fill the inner gap and clergy prepared to supply almost everything which is demanded by those who seek philosophical or religious products. Clergy has access to vulnerable people who are in search of meaning and happiness. Criminals who have infiltrated philosophical or religious groups can easily detect suitable victims. This situation is not confined to Buddhism.

The story where Jesus throws the money changers out of the temple is depicting a similar situation.

Buddhism offers help to people who experience stress and are in need of help. Meditation and other forms of religious activities are performed by genuinely devoted Buddhist and these individuals suffer because there are a few rotten apples in the congregation.

Abuse of power is made much easier in top-down

hierarchies, in particular when cover for rotten apples is provided from within the organisation.

Certain parts of the media may use bad examples of clergy to discredit religion or spiritual practice in general. This may leave people who are already disconnected from their own spiritual and religious background completely lost since there might be no spiritual or religious community left where they can turn to in times of need.

In Western societies some people turned to Asian religions and philosophies because they felt that somehow Judaism and Christianity did not help them.

Social contexts such as family, traditional religious groups and spontaneous interaction are neglected or even actively discouraged in certain modern societies or in particular situations such as in the Corona measures imposed.

Annotations to 'The Node and a Step Stone to Hell'

In the city of Wuppertal I was approached several times by people I did not know but somehow they felt that they should talk to me about issues relating to the time of the 3rd Reich in Wuppertal; I mean people in addition to the women I mention in the short story.

An old man started talking to me as I was taking pictures of the memorial which commemorates all the people who passed through Wuppertal on their way to concentration camps. This old man told me that he originally came from Czechoslovakia and that he was put on one of the trains heading to a concentration camp. At that time he was a young man and he survived the concentration camp but he lost all the other members of his family in camps.

After the war he had no choice but to stay in Germany because he had nowhere to go back to. He was now living close to Wuppertal because after the war he found out that his family members must have all passed through Wuppertal on their forced transportation to the concentration camps. He also witnessed outrageous cruelties performed against the passengers of these special trains which happened in Wuppertal at that time. He said that memories draw him back to this place. He pointed at the memorial and said this was really a tiny memorial. I agreed and said that I was told that the railway in Wuppertal had been a major crossing for the trains to several concentration camps. Then his train arrived, he said 'Good-bye, I hope that this will never be forgotten' and he boarded the train.

The memorial looks neglected, small and insignificant:

Photograph taken by Richard Grawath © 12th July 2015

A location of crimes against humanity in Wuppertal:

Photograph taken by Richard Grawath © 16th July 2015

The small train station Wuppertal–Steinbeck is the
place where trains stopped on the way to several

concentration camps. The memorial was erected in 1988 [30]. This means it took 43 years for the memorial to be erected. When I took the pictures it was hard to read the texts. How much effort would it be for the city of Wuppertal to make the letters easier to read? How about another memorial in a place which is more in the centre of the city and where more people would be made aware of the crimes against humanity?

The plaque of the memorial with the names of the destinations is incomplete and not correct:

Photograph taken by Richard Grawath © 16th July 2015

Recently it has been reported that Jewish people from Wuppertal were not sent to Riga [30]. For me the names of the remaining concentration camps on the table above still create sadness and anger about the crimes against humanity committed in Wuppertal. According to memorialmuseums.org more than 125 Jews were transported from Wuppertal to the concentration camp in Dachau [31]. The Dachau concentration camp is missing on the plaque of the memorial.

'Stolpersteine' are small bronze plaques placed in the pavement in front of the last known residence of a Jewish victim. These plaques list the name of the victim, the deportation date, the name of the concentration camp and also the date of the murder if the victim did not survive. There are also *Stolpersteine* for Holocaust survivors.

The *Stolpersteine* is a private initiative even though they are in a public place. These plaques are the art project of Gunter Demnig [32].

The boy commemorated by the Stolperstein in the picture below was 7 years old at the time of his deportation from Wuppertal:

Photograph taken by Richard Grawath © 12th July 2015

One woman told me that she still hears the souls of the victims who suffered during the 3rd Reich in Wuppertal. She said many citizens of Wuppertal knew about the transports and they knew that they could be cruel because there would not be any punishment for these cruelties.

In this short story I combined two stories because I thought that these stories somehow belong together.

I conducted some research about the story of the nurse since she gave me some details about the female dentist who had worked in the concentration camp. After the war the dentist worked as a dentist in one of the major cities in the north of Germany. I was also told that the dentist had not worked in that city before the war. Therefore I compared the lists of dentists working in that city during and shortly after the 3rd Reich. I found the name of a female dentist which fits the description but I cannot say that this is the dentist in question since I could not find her CV. The Holocaust survivor also told me that she tried to be heard as a witness during the Nuremberg trials but 'they' did not accept her as a witness. This Holocaust survivor said that she had written a witness statement and left it in a secure place so that future generations have a chance to read it.

When I wrote to Xavier Riaud because he had conducted research about the role of dentists experimenting with humans during the 3rd Reich [33] he replied that there were no female dentists on the list of dentists who experimented with humans but this list is not complete. The original study of Xavier Riaud was conducted in French but the link in the reference section refers to a shortened German translation [33].

Even though there were fewer female dentists compared to male dentists during the 3rd Reich I was surprised that there was not a single female dentist on the list. Did the Nazis edit the list at the end of the 3rd Reich?

On 29th July 2014 three men were throwing Molotov cocktails at the synagogue in Wuppertal [34]. In Wuppertal a lower court gave very mild sentences to the three guilty Palestinians and the rulings were later confirmed by a regional court although the suspended sentences were slightly extended [35]. The defendants claimed that firebombing the synagogue was not anti-Semitism but that it was an act of criticism of Israel's activities [35]. This claim of the defendants is not watertight since there are many peaceful ways of criticism and there was no justification for endangering the health and lives of people in this situation in Wuppertal. A current definition of anti-Semitism which has been adopted by the International Holocaust Remembrance Alliance could have led to better sentencing [36]. According to this current definition Jews do not have collective responsibility for activities of Israel as a state and acts are criminal when they target people or items that are Jewish, perceived to be Jewish or somehow connected to Jewish people [36].

Around that time there were also reports of anti-Semitic comments during demonstrations and none of these anti-Semitic shouts attracted the attention of the police or the courts [36].

The historical context of the attack on the synagogue in Wuppertal is important. In 1938 the synagogue was incinerated by anti-Semites in Wuppertal [37].

Anti-Semitism does not only occur in Germany. From 2017 to 2020 I was in the cafeteria and the main campus of the University of Malta where several times I heard anti-Semitic comments. My formal complaints were ignored and dismissed.

According to the chairman of the Jewish Cultural Association, Leonid Goldberg, anti-Semitism among young Moslems is on the increase [34]. The previous year it made global news when Shariah police tried to enforce Shariah law with respect to alcohol and gambling in Wuppertal [34].

Violent protest as performed above by the three men in Wuppertal is more likely to create negative publicity and is probably counterproductive to the pretended aim. Burning a place of worship or trying to burn a place of worship should never be acceptable regardless of the type of congregation.

The destruction of the Jewish Temple in Jerusalem by the Romans in ancient times is still in the memory of many people.

The other key issue is abuse of power at all levels. During the 3rd Reich power abuse from top to bottom was blatantly visible. Nowadays it is very blurred and most people are unable to spot the power abuse due to several reasons such as system conform propaganda by the established media, increased sophistication in public administration, cover-up strategies and the creation of fear.

Many members of the lower levels in society cannot handle the little power they have and they pick on individuals who they perceive as powerless to retaliate. At the higher levels power corrupts very fast and politicians who may have started their careers with the best of intentions soon end up indulging the accumulation of power and money.

Annotations to 'A Review: Paul Kuttner: An Endless Struggle'

I had an extensive exchange of letters with Paul and I also meet him several times. We never used German when we exchanged letters or discussed something.

There was no age differentiation between us even though I was much younger than Paul and we still discussed all sorts of issues. I am convinced that old age, high intelligence, education and experience are crucial for developing wisdom. Here I mean informal education since nowadays formal education is something pre-determined and often obtained through passing multiple-choice tests which have not much to do with real knowledge or even wisdom.

Paul also sent me a copy of his autobiography. It shows that Paul appreciated the dialogue across generations and I also enjoyed discussing all sorts of things with him. In the current society the separation of age groups is common practice, evident in assumptions about preferences and activities and I call this age segregation because this prevents the exchange of views and knowledge. Wisdom from older people is often not appreciated.

The concept of privacy is a good example. Many young people provide data about themselves to websites and later they are surprised when they find out that it is difficult to delete private information from the public domain.

In his letters to me Paul was still writing about the loss of his family members during the Holocaust. Paul was convinced that his murdered family members have reached immortality through his book and through public memorials such as the Stolpersteine. He said that Hitler wanted to turn humans into numbers by assigning numbers to humans in concentration camps, but in the end Hitler failed. There is a terrible parallel: technocrats see humans just as numbers which can be used and disregarded after use. For Paul humans are individuals with names and stories.

Paul was part of loosely organised circles which included individuals from England and the USA, Russian and Jewish immigrants, and their descendants. I was introduced to some of them and lively discussions occurred. Frequently different opinions were exchanged without creating any bad feelings. This is something which current society, the established media and the politicians of most established parties lack.

References

1. Stainton-Rogers, Wendy. Logics of Enquiry. [book auth.] Stephen Potter. *Doing Postgraduate Research.* London : Sage, 2008, pp. 73-91.

2. Introduction to Probability. [book auth.] David F Groebner, et al. *Business Statistics A Decision Making Approach.* Upper Saddle River : Prentice Hall Pearson, 2011, pp. 170-214.

3. Bennett, Maxwell and Hacker, Peter. The Argument Selections from Philosophical Foundations of Neuroscience. [book auth.] Maxwel Bennett, et al. *Neuroscience and Philosophy: Brain, Mind, and Language.* New York : Columbia University Press, 2007, pp. 3-48.

4. Andrade, Jackie. Consciousness Chapter 15. [book auth.] Nick Braisby and Angus Gellatly. *Cognitive Psychology.* Oxford : Oxford University Press, 2005, pp. 545-577.

5. Despopoulos, Agamemnon and Silbernagel, Stefan. Chapter 3 Autonomic Nervous System (ANS). *Color Atlas of Physiology.* Stuttgart, New York : Georg Thieme Verlag, 2003, pp. 78-87.

6. —. Chapter 8 Cardiovascular System. *Color Atlas of Physiology.* Stuttgart, New York : Georg Thieme Verlag, 2003, pp. 186-221.

7. Barral, Jean-Pierre and Croibier, Alain. Chapter 22 - Vagus Nerve. *Manual Therapy for the Cranial Nerves.* 2009, pp. 191-207.

8. Despopoulos, Agamemnon and Silbernagel, Stefan. Chapter 12 Central Nervous System and Senses. *Color Atlas of Physiology.* Stuttgart, New York : Georg Thieme Verlag, 2003, pp. 310-371.

9. Despopulos, Agamemnon and Silbernagel, Stefan. Chapter 2 Nerve and Muscle, Physical Work. *Color Atlas of Physiology.* Stuttgart, New York : Georg Thieme, 2003, pp. 42-87.

10. Ruiz, Ramon. *History and Evolution of the Scientific Thought.* Culiacan, Sinaloa, Mexico : s.n., 2006.

11. Magner, Lois N. *A History of Medicine.* London, New York : Taylor & Francis, 2005.

12. Sheldrake, Rupert. *Science Set Free.* New York : Crown Publishing Group, 2012.

13. Greenberg, Daniel S. *Science for Sale - The Perils, Rewards, and Delusions of Campus Capitalism.* Chicago, London : The University of Chicago Press, 2007.

14. Arthur, Charles. The onco-mouse that did not roar. *New Scientist.* [Online] June 26, 1993. https://www.newscientist.com/article/mg13818790-300-the-onco-mouse-that-didnt-roar/.

15. Stallwood, Adrian. *Science Corrupted - Revealed: The Nightmare World of GM Mice.* Tonbridge, Kent : Animal Aid, 2013.

16. *House Dust Mite - The Paradox.* Cinteza, Mircea and Daian, Cristina. 4, 2014, Maedica A Journal of Clinical Medicine, Vol. 9, pp. 313-315.

17. *Lead toxicity: a review.* Wani, Ab L, Ara, A and Usmani, Jawed A. 2015, Interdiscip Toxicol, Vol. 8, pp. 55-64.

18. *Cadmium toxicity and treatment: An update.* Rafati, Rahimzadeh, et al. 3, 2017, Caspian J Intern Med, Vol. 8, pp. 135-145.

19. Clapp, Richard, et al. *The American People's Dioxin Report.* Falls Church, VA : Center For Health, Environment and Justice, 1999.

20. Claesson, Frida. *Literature survey of Dioxins and Poly Aromatic Hydrocarbons in combination with waste combustion.* Gothenburg : University College of Borås, Åbo Akademi, University of Gothenburg, 2008.

21. *Polymer Flammability Final Report.* Washington DC : US Department of Transportation, 2005.

22. Hull, Richard T and Stec, Anna A. *Fire Retardancy of Polymers: New Strategies and Mechanisms.* Cambridge : Royal Society of Chemistry, 2009.

23. *Acute toluene intoxication–clinical presentation, management and prognosis: a prospective observational study.* Camara-Lemarroy, Carlos R, et al. 2015, BMC Emergency Medicine, pp. 1-7.

24. Vitale, C M and Gutovitz, S. Aromatic (Benzene, Toluene) Toxicity. [Online] January 2020. [Cited: October 12, 2020.] https://www.ncbi.nlm.nih.gov/books/NBK532257/#_NBK532257_pubdet_.

25. National Center for Biotechnology Information. PubChem Compound Summary for CID 313, Hydrochloric acid. *PubChem.* [Online] 2020. [Cited: October 12, 2020.] https://pubchem.ncbi.nlm.nih.gov/compound/Hydrochloric-acid.

26. Kovler, K. Radioactive Materials. *Toxicity of Building Materials.* 2012.

27. Ehrlich, Richard S. Thailand tackles its bad boy Buddhist monks. *AsiaTimes.com.* [Online] August 14, 2018. https://asiatimes.com/2018/08/thailand-tackles-its-bad-boy-buddhist-monks/.

28. Agence France-Presse, in Bangkok. Monks' bad behaviour hotline launched by Thai Buddhist authorities. *the guardian.com.* [Online] June 19, 2014.
https://www.theguardian.com/world/2014/jun/19/mo nks-bad-behaviour-hotline-thai-buddhist-authorities.

29. Lewis, Craig. Buddhist monk arrested in bodh gaya for alleged physical and sexual abuse of 15 novice monks. *Buddhistdoor Global.* [Online] September 3, 2018.
https://www.buddhistdoor.net/news/buddhist-monk-arrested-in-bodh-gaya-for-alleged-physical-and-sexual-abuse-of-15-novice-monks.

30. Denkmal-Wuppertal. Mahnmal zur Erinnerung an die Deportation jüdischer Mitbürger vom Bahnhof Steinbeck. [Online] May 17, 2010. [Cited: December 11, 2014.] http://www.denkmal-wuppertal.de/2010/05/mahnmal-zur-erinnerung-die-deportation.html.

31. Gedenkstaettenportal zu Orten der Erinnerung in Europa. B. *Wuppertal Old Synagogue Community Centre, History.* [Online] [Cited: September 15, 2020.]
https://www.memorialmuseums.org/eng/denkmaeler/view/13/Wuppertal-Old-Synagogue-Community-Centre.

32. Kuttner, Paul. *An Endless Struggle.* 1st. Edn.: Vantage Press Publ., 2010. ISBN 978-0-533-15498-2.

33. Riaud, Xavier. Studie der zahnmedizinischen Praxis und ihrer Entartungen in den Konzentrationslagern Nazideutschlands. [Online] Centre François Viète . [Cited: December 14, 2014.] http://www.histoire-medecine.fr/seconde-

guerre-mondiale-studie-der-zahnmedizinischen-praxis-und-entartungen-in-den-konzentrationslagern-nazideutschlands.php.

34. Poehle, Sven. 'Pure anti-Semitism' behind synagogue attack, says Wuppertal Jewish leader. *dw.com/en.* [Online] January 25, 2015. [Cited: September 15, 2020.] https://www.dw.com/en/pure-anti-semitism-behind-synagogue-attack-says-wuppertal-jewish-leader/a-18216819.

35. Weinthal, Benjamin. German court calls synagogue torching an act to 'criticize Israel'. *The Jerusalem Post.* [Online] January 13, 2017. [Cited: September 15, 2020.] https://www.jpost.com/diaspora/german-court-calls-synagogue-torching-an-act-to-criticize-israel-478330.

36. Näegele, Benjamin. Judge Rules Wuppertal Synagogue Firebombing Was Not Anti-Semitic, So What Happened? [Online] January 17, 2017. https://www.bnaibrith.org/expert-analysis/judge-rules-wuppertal-synagogue-firebombing-was-not-anti-semitic-so-what-happened.

37. Gedenkstaettenportal zu Orten der Erinnerung in Europa. A. Wuppertal Old Synagogue Community Centre, Introduction. [Online] Stiftung Denkmal fuer die ermordeten Juden Europas. [Cited: September 15, 2020.] https://www.memorialmuseums.org/eng/denkmaeler/view/13/Wuppertal-Old-Synagogue-Community-Centre.

www.ingramcontent.com/pod-product-compliance
Lightning Source LLC
Chambersburg PA
CBHW070123290526
45789CB00005B/2124